100 facts
ANCIENT ROME

100 facts

ANCIENT ROME

Fiona Macdonald

Consultant: Rupert Matthews

Miles Kelly

First published in 2001 by Miles Kelly Publishing Ltd
Harding's Barn, Bardfield End Green, Thaxted, Essex, CM6 3PX, UK

Copyright © Miles Kelly Publishing Ltd 2001

This edition updated 2014, printed 2018

12 14 15 13

Publishing Director Belinda Gallagher
Creative Director Jo Cowan
Editorial Director Rosie Neave
Designers Rob Hale, Andrea Slane
Image Manager Liberty Newton
Indexer Jane Parker
Production Elizabeth Collins, Jennifer Brunwin-Jones
Reprographics Stephan Davis, Jennifer Cozens, Thom Allaway
Assets Lorraine King

ISBN 978-1-78209-586-6

Printed in China

British Library Cataloguing-in-Publication Data
A catalogue record for this book is available from the British Library

ACKNOWLEDGEMENTS

The publishers would like to thank the following sources for the use of their photographs:
Key: t = top, b = bottom, c = centre, l = left, r = right, bg = background, rt = repeated throughout

Cover (front) stephen Mulcahey/Alamy, (back, t) WDG Photo, (back, l) I. Pilon
Alamy 8(b) Caro; 14(cr) The Art Archive **Art Archive** 10(tl) DeA Picture Library **Corbis** 6–7 Vanni Archive;
20(bl) Roger Wood; 21(tr) Mimmo Jodice; 30(bl) Alfredo Dagli Orti/The Art Archive; 31 Farrell Grehan; 42 Araldo de Luca;
43 Richard Baker/In Pictures; 46 Arne Hodalic; 47 Roger Ressmeyer **Dover** 20–21(tc) **Shutterstock** 2–3 Laurence
Gough; 5(tc) and 47(r) jps, 5(b) Iakov Kalinin; 6(heading panel rt) Anelina, (fact panel rt) PaulPaladin; 6–7(label panels)
Pakhnyushcha; 7(caption panel) David M. Schrader; 8(heading panel rt) Konstanttin; 8–9(bg) Vitaly Korovin; 9(fact panel)
Apostrophe, (b)Filip Fuxa; 10(heading panel) haveseen, (caption panel rt) Valentin Agapov; 10–11(bg) Luba V Nel; 13 Ariy,
(fact panel cl) Jaywarren79, (b+bg rt) Ev Thomas; 14(heading panel rt) aopsan; 14–15(panel bgs) Vitaly Korovin, (tc) Yulia
Davidovich, (tr) Dionisvera; 15(herbs & spices, clockwise from tl) Noraluca013, Imageman, Robyn Mackenzie, Madlen,
Volosina, (vegetables, clockwise from tl) Vladyslav Danilin, Valentyn Volkov, Dulce Rubia, Jiang Hongyan, Madlen,
eye-blink, (cr) picturepartners; 16–17(bg) Tischenko Irina, (br) James Steidl, (b) Bill McKelvie; 17(c, rt) Lora liu; 18(heading
panel) Valentin Agapov; 18–19(bg rt) Andre Viegas; 23(flowers, herbs & spices, clockwise from tl) M.Khebra, Aleksandra
Duda, Africa Studio, Eric Gevaert; 24–25(bg) mg1408; 24(t); 25(tr) Viacheslav Lopatin; 28(heading panel rt) Vitaly Korovin;
29(t panel) ImageState, (tr) Iakov Kalinin; 30(l panel) donatas1205; 31(br, top to bottom) Paul Picone, Chris Hill, I. Pilon,
(tr panel) Molodec; 32–33(bg) Javier Rosano; 34 Piotr Zajc; 36–37(bg) javarman; 38–39(bg) RoyStudio.eu;
42–43(bg) donatas1205; 42(panel t) bomg, (panel c) Clipart deSIGN; 44 JeniFoto, 46–47 khd
Superstock 11 imagebroker.net; 15 DeAgostini; 22(tr) Universal Images Group; 27(br) Album/Prisma/Album;
30–31(t) Universal Images Group; 35 DeAgostini; 36 DeAgostini; 37 J.D. Dallet/age fotostock; 39 Image Asset
Management Ltd.; 41 Robert Harding Picture Library **Topfoto** 18–19(tc) AAAC; 19(cr) The Granger Collection;
27(bl) The Granger Collection; 31(bl) The Granger Collection

All other photographs are from:
digitalSTOCK, digitalvision, Dreamstime.com, Fotolia.com, iStockphoto.com,
John Foxx, PhotoAlto, PhotoDisc, PhotoEssentials, PhotoPro, Stockbyte

All artworks are from the Miles Kelly Artwork Bank

Every effort has been made to acknowledge the source and copyright holder of each picture.
Miles Kelly Publishing apologizes for any unintentional errors or omissions.

Made with paper from a sustainable forest

www.mileskelly.net

Contents

The centre of an empire 6

Capital city 8

Home sweet home 10

Buying and selling 12

Eating and drinking 14

School days 16

Family life 18

Roman style 20

Looking good 22

Bath time 24

Having fun 26

Let the games begin 28

Ruling Rome 30

In the army 32

Ruled by Rome 34

The farming life 36

Work like a slave 38

Roman know-how 40

Prayers and sacrifices 42

On the move 44

Uncovering the past 46

Index 48

The centre of an empire

River Tiber
This was a source of water for the people of Rome

Circus Maximus
A huge stadium built to stage public entertainment.

Imperial Palace
First built around AD 30 the palace remained in use for 300 years

Temple of the Divine Claudius
A temple dedicated to the patron gods of the imperial family

1 The Italian city of Rome was once the hub of one of the world's greatest empires. An empire is made up of lots of countries governed by one ruler. Around 1000 BC Rome was a village on the River Tiber, but it soon grew rich and powerful. It was busy and exciting, with many beautiful buildings. By 200 BC the Romans ruled most of Italy, and started to invade neighbouring lands.

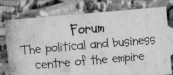

Forum
The political and business centre of the empire

Temple of Apollo
The Greek god Apollo became popular in Rome in later years

Colosseum
Famous amphitheatre where gladiatorial fights were staged

Baths of Trajan
Built by the Emperor Trajan as a place of relaxation for citizens

Ludus Magnus
Training school and barracks for gladiators who fought in the Colosseum

Servian Wall
The stone wall around Rome built around 490 BC. It was replaced by the larger Aurelian Wall in about AD 275 and was allowed to fall into ruin

Aqua Claudia
Aqueduct that brought fresh water to Rome from springs 72 kilometres to the southeast

▲ The Forum was the central hub of Rome. It was the home of government and a busy marketplace. The rest of the city contained places for leisure, sport and religion, and was filled with houses and blocks of flats where the citizens lived.

Capital city

2 **Over one million people lived in Rome.** By around AD 300, Rome was the largest city in the world. There were citizens who could vote and serve in the army, and there were non-citizens who did not have these rights. The government was run by wealthy nobles and knights. Plebeians (ordinary people) were usually fairly poor but were citizens of Rome. Slaves were non-citizens. They were not free to leave their owners and had no rights.

▼ In 44 BC the dictator Julius Caesar built the Curia Julia as a meeting house for the Senate of Rome. The building later became a church and has survived intact to the present day.

3 **The Forum was the centre of Rome.** It was originally an open space at the foot of the Capitoline Hill, and was used as a market place, meeting place and picnic area. Later, government buildings were erected here, including offices for the Senate, law courts and temples.

Aurelian Wall

Servian Wall

4 Rome was very well protected. It was surrounded by 50 kilometres of strong stone walls to keep out attackers. Visitors had to enter the city through one of its 37 gates, which were guarded by soldiers and watchmen.

◀ In AD 275 the old Servian Wall of about 380 BC was replaced by the Aurelian Wall that protected the new, larger city of Rome. The new wall was 19 kilometres long, 16 metres tall and had 383 towers. It remained in use until the siege of 1870.

6 Rome relied on its drains. The city was so crowded that without good drains the citizens could have caught diseases from sewage and died. The largest sewer, called the *cloaca maxima*, was so high and wide that a horse and cart could drive through it.

I DON'T BELIEVE IT!

Roman engineers also designed public lavatories. They were convenient but not at all private – users had to sit on rows of seats, side by side!

5 The Romans were great water engineers. They designed aqueducts (raised channels to carry water from streams in distant hills and mountains to the city). The homes of rich citizens were supplied with running water carried in lead pipes. Ordinary people had to drink from public fountains.

▶ The Romans built the Pont Du Gard in the south of France – a 360-metre-long aqueduct supported on three tiers of arches.

Home sweet home

▲ A reconstruction of a house belonging to a rich family in the city of Pompeii. This grand room, the Atrium, was where guests were entertained.

QUIZ

1. What were Roman blocks of flats known as?

2. What are pictures made with coloured stones or glass called?

3. How did Romans heat their homes?

Answers:
1. Insulae 2. Mosaics
3. Wealthy families had underfloor heating, ordinary families used fires

7 Rich Romans had more than one home. Rome was noisy, dirty and smelly. Wealthy citizens would often have a house just outside the city (a *villa urbana*), or a big house with land in the country (a *villa rustica*) in which they spent the summer months.

8 **The Romans built the world's first high-rise apartments.** Most of the people who lived in Ostia, a busy port close to Rome, had jobs connected with trade, such as shipbuilders and money-changers. They lived in blocks of flats known as *insulae*. A typical block was three or four storeys high, with up to 100 small, dirty, crowded rooms.

▼ On the ground floor of an *insula* were shops, and on the first floor were flats and apartments for families. The poorest families lived in single rooms on the top floor.

10 **Many homes had a pool, but it wasn't used for swimming!** Decorative pools were built in the central courtyards of large homes, surrounded by plants and statues. Some had fountains. In others mosaics (pictures made of tiny coloured stones or squares of glass) covered the floor.

11 **Rome's fire brigade was made up of specially trained freed slaves.** People who could not afford central heating warmed their rooms with fires in clay pots, which often set houses alight.

9 **Wealthy family homes had underfloor central heating.** Blasts of hot air, warmed by a wood-burning furnace, circulated in channels built beneath the floor. Slaves chopped wood and stoked the fire.

▶ Some public buildings and wealthy homes had a heating system called a hypocaust. Hot air from a fire tended by a slave passed through spaces under the floor and up the walls to keep the rooms warm.

Space in walls for hot air to circulate

Fire in basement

Space under floor for hot air to circulate

Buying and selling

12 **Roman ships travelled the known world.** Merchants sailed around the Empire and beyond looking for trade. Ships reached as far as India to the east and Iceland to the north. Luxury goods, such as silk, spices and furs, were the most sought after.

▼ A Roman ship approaches Dubris (now Dover) in Britain in AD 90 as a lighthouse is built on the cliff to help guide ships into harbour.

QUIZ

1. How many levels was Trajan's Market built on?

2. Who wore jewellery in ancient Rome – men or women?

3. Did Roman ships sail to Iceland?

Answers:
1. Five 2. Both men and women wore jewellery 3. Yes – they sailed there to trade

▼ Each archway in Trajan's Market in Rome housed a shop or fast food stall. It is thought that the larger ground floor arches may have been offices for government officials.

13 Rome housed the world's first shopping mall. It was called Trajan's Market, and was built on five different levels on the slopes of the Quirinal Hill in the centre of Rome. It contained over 150 different shops together with a large main hall.

14 Romans liked a bargain. Most prices were not fixed, and customers haggled with sellers until they agreed on a price. Shopping could be hard work – different types of goods were sold in different areas of the city, and many shops and stalls opened early and closed at noon.

▼ Both men and women wore jewellery in ancient Rome. Some pieces indicated the rank and wealth of the wearer, but most were simply decorative.

Necklace
A necklace made of coloured glass strung on wire was a relatively cheap but impressive piece

Ring
A costly gold ring set with a stone

Bracelet
A bracelet made of the black stone jet

Earrings
A pair of expensive gold earrings in the shape of dolphins

Eating and drinking

15 Most Romans ate little during the day. They had bread and water for breakfast and a snack of bread, cheese or fruit around midday. The main meal was eaten in the late afternoon, and in rich households it had three courses. Poor people ate simple food: soups made with lentils and onions, barley porridge, peas, cabbage and cheap cuts of meat stewed in vinegar.

Grapes

Figs

▲ Romans ate large quantities of fruit raw, cooked or dried. Grapes were crushed and made into wine.

ROMAN FOOD

Patina de piris (Pear soufflé)

Ingredients:
1 kg pears (peeled and cored)
6 eggs (beaten)   4 tbsp honey
oil   pinch of salt   ½ tsp cumin
ground pepper to taste

Ask an adult to help you with this recipe. Mash the pears together with the pepper, cumin, honey, and a bit of oil. Add the beaten eggs and put into a casserole dish. Cook for approximately 30 minutes in a moderate oven. Serve with a little pepper sprinkled on top.

► An engraved drinking cup made in Gaul, France, in about AD 380. The skills of making glass were lost after the fall of Rome.

16 Only rich people had their own kitchen. They could afford to employ a chef with slaves to help him. Ordinary people went to *popinae* (cheap eating houses) for their main meal, or bought ready-cooked snacks from roadside fast food stalls.

▲ Herbs and spices added flavour to dishes. Pepper and coriander came from across the Indian Ocean and were very expensive.

Oregano

Black pepper

Juniper berries

Coriander seeds

Thyme

Garlic

Olives

Asparagus

Celery

Lentils

Radishes

▲ Vegetables were eaten raw or cooked in stews. Garlic was a favourite ingredient used in many dishes.

Sardine

17 At parties, the Romans ate lying down. Men and women lay on long couches arranged around a table. They also often wore crowns of flowers, and took off their sandals before entering the dining room.

▲ Fish and meat were relatively expensive so poorer people rarely ate them. Sardines could be dried and salted for storage.

▼ A relief shows a rich woman reclining on a couch with her child while a slave or servant brings in a dish of food.

School days

18 Roman boys learned to speak well. At school they were taught reading, maths and public speaking – skills they would need in their careers. There were no newspapers or TVs, so politicians, army leaders and government officials had to make speeches to explain their plans and policies to Roman crowds.

▼ Boys attended school from seven years old. At 16, their education was complete.

19 Roman girls did not go to school. They stayed at home, where their mothers or women slaves taught them household tasks, such as how to cook, clean, weave cloth and look after children. Girls from wealthy families, or families who ran a business, also learned to read, write and keep accounts.

20 Many of the best teachers were slaves. Schoolmasters and private tutors often came from Greece. They were purchased by wealthy people who wanted to give their sons a good education. The Greeks had a long tradition of learning, which the Romans admired.

▼ An inscription in Latin placed over the doorway of a house. It means 'Peace to those coming in'.

PAX·INTRANTIBVS
SALVS·EXEVNTIBVS

21 **The Romans did not write on paper.** They used thin slices of wood for letters and day-to-day business. For notes Romans used flat, wooden boards covered with wax, as the wax could be smoothed over and used again. For important documents that they wanted to keep, they used cleaned, polished calfskin or papyrus.

Ink pot

Pens

Stylus, to use with a wax tablet

Wax tablet

22 **Romans made ink from soot.** Black ink was a mixture of soot, vinegar and a sticky gum that oozed from tree bark. Some Roman writing has survived for almost 2000 years.

▶ A list of Roman words and their English meanings. Some modern words are based on Roman words. For instance the word 'library' comes from *liber*.

ROMAN	ENGLISH
EPISTOLA	LETTER
VELLUM	CALFSKIN
GRAMMATICUS	SCHOOLMASTER
PAEDAGOGUS	PRIVATE TUTOR
STYLUS	WRITING STICK
BIBLIOTHECA	LIBRARY
LIBER	BOOK
LIBRARII	SLAVES WHO WORKED IN A LIBRARY

▲ Quick notes were scribbled on a wax tablet and wiped clean later. More important messages were written in ink onto vellum (calfskin parchment).

24 **Many Romans read standing up.** It took time and patience to learn how to read from a papyrus scroll. Most were at least 10 metres long. Readers held the scroll in their right hand, a stick in their left, and unrolled a small section of the scroll at a time.

23 **Many boys did not go to school.** Poorer boys who needed to earn a living would get a job in a workshop or on a farm. They learned how to run a business or carry out a trade. At 16 they might set up in business on their own.

Family life

25 **A Roman father had the power of life and death over his family.** By law each family was led by a man – usually the oldest surviving male. He was known as the *paterfamilias* (father of a family). The house and its contents belonged to him. He had the right to punish any family members who misbehaved – even his mother and other older female relatives.

▶ A Roman wedding. The bride and groom hold hands while their families watch. Most marriages were arranged by the families for business or political reasons. The couple being married had little say in the decision.

26 **Families included more than blood relations.** To the Romans, the word 'family' meant all the people living and working together in the same household. So families included many different slaves and servants, as well as a husband, wife and their children.

◀ The Romans gave a good luck charm, called a *bulla*, to their babies.

I DON'T BELIEVE IT!

The Romans invented Valentine's Day, but called it Lupercalia. Boys picked a girl's name from a hat, and she was meant to be their girlfriend for the year!

27 **Life in Rome was easier if you were a boy.**
Boys were valued because they would carry on the family name, and might bring fame and honour to a family through their careers. For Roman girls, childhood was short. They were often married by the age of 12, and many had become mothers by the time they were 15.

28 **Families liked to keep pets.** Many statues and paintings show children playing with animals. Dogs, cats and doves were all popular. Some families also kept ornamental fish and tame deer.

▶ Roman women play with a fawn (young deer), while enjoying a day in the countryside.

29 **Funerals were very elaborate.** A funeral was a chance for a family to show off to their friends and neighbours. Huge feasts were provided, speeches were made and actors played out incidents from the life of the dead person.

◀ Some Romans cremated their dead. The ashes were then put in an urn before being buried, often in a family tomb.

19

Roman style

30 Most Roman clothes were made without sewing. Loose-fitting robes made of long strips of cloth were draped round the body and held in place by pins, brooches or belts. Most women wore layers – a *tunica* (thin shift), a *stola* (long, sleeveless dress), and a *palla* (cloak). Men wore a *colobium* (knee-length tunic) with a semi-circular cloak called a toga over the top.

▶ Three different ways that women could wear the *palla*, which was often made of costly fabric.

31 Clothes were different depending on how important you were. Ordinary men wore plain white togas, but government leaders, called senators, appeared in togas with a purple stripe around the edge. Rich men and women wore robes made of smooth, fine-quality wool and silk. Ordinary people's clothes were much rougher.

◀ This mosaic shows a man wearing a toga. The toga could be worn only by men who were citizens of Rome. Many men had a special toga of costly coloured linen to wear at special events.

▶ A gold fibula, or pin. These small pins were used to hold cloaks and tunics in place.

32 **Clothes told the world who you were.** People from many different cultures lived in lands ruled by Rome, and they wore different styles of clothes. Men from Egypt wore wigs and linen kilts. Celtic women from northern Europe wore long, woollen shawls, woven in brightly coloured checks. Celtic men wore trousers.

TOGA TIME!

1. Ask an adult for a blanket or sheet. White is best, like the Romans.
2. Drape the sheet over your left shoulder. Now pass the rest behind your back.
3. Pull the sheet across your front, so that you're wrapped up in it.
4. Finally, drape the last end over your right hund and there you have it, a Roman toga!

◀ Sandals known as *crepidae* were worn by men and women all year round.

33 **Boots were made for walking!** Soldiers and travellers wore lace-up boots with thick leather soles studded with iron nails. Other footwear included *socci*, loose-fitting slippers to wear indoors. Farmers wore shoes made of a single piece of ox-hide wrapped round the foot, called *carbatinae*. There were also *crepidae* – comfortable lace-up sandals with open toes.

▲ These Roman sandals have metal studs in the soles to make sure that they don't wear down too quickly.

21

Looking good

34 **Roman hairstyles changed according to fashion.** All free-born women grew their hair long, as short hair was a sign of slavery. In early Roman times plain and simple styles were fashionable. Later on, most women wore their hair tied back. Men usually wore their hair short, and were mostly clean shaven.

▲ Hairstyle fashions changed frequently. This lady's style dates to about AD 90.

35 **The Romans painted their faces.** They admired pale, smooth skin. Women, and some men, used stick-on patches of cloth called *splenia* to cover spots, and wore make-up. They used crushed chalk or white lead as face-powder, red ochre (crumbly earth) for blusher, plant juice for lipstick and wood-ash or powdered antimony (a silvery metal) as eye-liner.

◄ Most rich women had slaves whose job it was to keep their hair perfect.

36 Blonde hair was highly prized. Most Romans had wiry, dark-brown hair, so delicate, blonde hair was admired by fashionable people because it was unusual. Women used vinegar and lye (an early form of soap, made from urine and wood-ash) to bleach their own hair.

37 Romans liked to smell sweet. Olive oil was rubbed into the skin to cleanse and soften, then scraped off with a curved metal tool. Ingredients for perfume came from many different lands – flowers from southern Europe, spices from India and Africa, and sweet-smelling bark and resin from Arabia.

Roses to make perfume

Star anise to make perfume

Saffron for eyeshadow

Herbs such as majoram to make perfume

▲ Many plants were used to make perfume and cosmetics.

39 Tonsors (Roman barbers) did more than shave. They worked in small shops, and passed on news and gossip about famous people, so some men went every day to catch up on the latest events. A boy's first shave – his *tonsora* – was a sign that he was an adult man.

38 Combs were made from bone, ivory or wood. Like combs today, they were designed to smooth and untangle hair, and were sometimes worn as hair ornaments. But they had another, less pleasant, purpose – they were used for combing out all the little nits and lice!

▲ Fine combs such as this teased out tangles and removed pests.

Bath time

▼ The Roman baths at Bath, in Somerset. Only the actual water bath is original, the other buildings date from the 18th century.

40 **The Romans went to public baths to relax.** These huge buildings were more than just places to get clean. They were also fitness centres and meeting places. Visitors could take part in sports, such as wrestling, do exercises, have a massage or a haircut. They could buy scented oils and perfumes, read books, eat snacks or admire works of art in the bath's own sculpture gallery!

41 **Men and women could not bathe together.** Women usually went to the baths in the mornings, while most men were at work. Men went to the baths in the afternoons.

I DON'T BELIEVE IT!

Although the Romans liked bathing, they visited the baths only once in every nine days. Basins of water were used in between baths to wash hands or faces.

42 Bathing wasn't simple – there were lots of stages.

First bathers sat in a very hot room full of steam. Then they went into a hot, dry room, where a slave removed all the sweat and dirt from their skin, using a metal scraper and olive oil. To cool off, they went for a swim in a tepid pool. Finally, they jumped into a bracing cold pool.

▼ The Baths of Caracalla in Rome included not only baths but libraries, shops and gardens that covered a total of 25 hectares.

② *Tepidarium*
Cool or tepid pool

① *Caldarium*
Hot room

③ *Frigidarium*
Coldest pool

Fires heat the water for the hot rooms

▲ Roman baths were open to anyone who paid the entrance fee. They were one of the few areas where rich and poor mixed freely. Some baths had two sections, one for men and one for women, but most baths had days for men and days for women.

25

Having fun

43 Roman theatre-goers preferred comedies to tragedies. Comic plays had happy endings, and made audiences laugh. Tragedies were serious, and ended with misery and suffering. The Romans also liked clowns, and invented mime, a story told without words, through dance and movement.

▼ All the parts in Roman plays were performed by men. For women's roles, men wore masks and dressed in female costume. Women could not be actors, except in mime.

Stages were backed by permanent walls of stone with doorways and balconies that could be used to represent temples and houses

The front of the stage was called the *pulpitum*. Actors stood here to make important speeches

Theatres had no roofs, so audiences were not undercover. Plays took place only during the day when there was enough light

44 Plays were originally part of religious festivals. Many dramas showed scenes from myths and legends, and were designed to make people think about morals. Later, plays were written on all sorts of topics – including politics. Some were paid for by rich politicians, to spread their message. They gave free tickets to Roman citizens, hoping to win votes.

45

Theatres were huge and well-built. The theatre at Orange in France seats almost 10,000 people and is so cleverly designed that even people in the back row can hear the actors.

Seats were made of hard stone, but sometimes people could hire soft cushions to sit on

46

Actors wore masks to help audiences see what each character was feeling. They were carved and painted in bright colours, with large features and exaggerated expressions of happiness, sadness or fright.

47

The Romans liked music and dancing. Groups of buskers played in the streets, or could be hired for parties. Among ordinary families, favourite instruments included pipes, castanets, flutes, cymbals and horns. Rich, educated people preferred the gentler sound of the lyre, which was played to accompany poets and singers.

48

People enjoyed games of skill and chance. Adults and children played dice and knucklebones, which needed nimble fingers. They played a game similar to draughts, which relied on luck and quick thinking. Sometimes bets were made on who would win.

▶ Six-sided dice were made of bone or ivory. They were shaken in a round pot before being thrown.

◀ Masks worn by Roman actors as shown in a mosaic from Rome. The male mask was used for comedy, the female for tragedy.

Let the games begin

49 **Gladiators were admired for their strength, skill and bravery.** These men were sent into an arena (an open space with tiered seats on all sides) to fight. Most gladiators would be killed or badly injured in the arena.

▶ Different types of gladiator had special equipment and fought in ways governed by strict rules, which were enforced by a referee.

Secutor

Samnite

Hoplomachus

50 **Most gladiators didn't choose to fight.** They were prisoners of war or criminals condemned to fight in the arena. Some men volunteered as gladiators to gain fame and wealth. Success could bring riches and freedom.

I DON'T BELIEVE IT!

Some gladiators became so popular that people used to write graffiti about them on the walls of buildings around Rome!

51 **Gladiators fought wild beasts.** Animals such as lions, tigers and crocodiles were brought from distant parts of the Empire to be hunted by gladiators in the arena. Sometimes criminals with no weapons were put into the arena along with the wild animals. They did not last long.

52 The Colosseum was an amazing building for its time. Also known as the Flavian Amphitheatre, it was a huge oval arena in the centre of Rome, used for gladiator fights and the executions of criminals. It opened in AD 80, and could seat 50,000 people. It was built of stone, concrete and marble and had 80 separate entrances.

▼ The Colosseum was the largest amphitheatre in the Roman empire.

► Chariot drivers wore helmets, but no other protective clothing.

54 Chariots often collided and overturned. Each charioteer carried a sharp knife, called a *falx*, to cut himself free from the wreckage. Even so, many horses and charioteers were killed.

53 Some Romans liked a day at the races. Horses pulled fast chariots round racetracks, called 'circuses'. The most famous was the Circus Maximus in Rome, which could hold 250,000 spectators. There could be up to 24 races each day. Twelve chariots took part in each race, running seven times round the oval track – a total distance of about 8 kilometres.

55 Racing rivalries sometimes led to riots. Races were organized by four separate teams – the Reds, Blues, Greens and Whites. Charioteers wore tunics in their team colours. Each team had a keen – and violent – group of fans.

Ruling Rome

56 According to legend, the first king, Romulus, came to power in 753 BC. Six kings ruled after him, but they were unjust and cruel. After King Tarquin the Proud was overthrown in 509 BC, Rome became a republic (a state without a king). Every year the people elected two consuls (senior lawyers) to head the government. Other officials were elected too. The republic lasted for over 400 years.

▼ Caesar's power and ambition angered his political opponents, and a group of them assassinated him.

57 In 47 BC a successful general called Julius Caesar declared himself dictator. This meant that he wanted to rule on his own for life. Many people feared that he was trying to end the republic, and rule like the old kings. Caesar was murdered in 44 BC by his political enemies. After this, there were many years of civil war.

▲ Legend says the twins Romulus and Remus were suckled by a wolf before being rescued by a shepherd.

I DON'T BELIEVE IT!

Some Roman emperors were mad and even dangerous. Emperor Nero was said to have laughed and played music while watching a terrible fire that destroyed a large part of Rome.

▲ This relief shows the emperor Trajan speaking to his army in AD 106. By this date emperors would command the army in battle and were expected to be talented generals.

58 In 27 BC Caesar's nephew Octavian seized power in Rome. He declared himself 'First Citizen', and said he would bring back peace and good government to Rome. He ended the civil war, and introduced many strong new laws. But he also changed the Roman government forever. He took a new name, 'Augustus', and became the first emperor of Rome.

59 Later the army took over. In 193 Emperor Commodus was murdered and the senate met to decide who would take over. The army marched to Rome and made Septimus Severus emperor. After this it was the army who decided who would be emperor.

Emperor Caligula
AD 12–41

Emperor Nero
AD 37–68

Emperor Constantine
280–337

◄ The emperors put their portraits on coins to remind everyone who was in charge of the empire.

◄ The Roman general Octavian Caesar ruled Rome from 27 BC to AD 14.

31

In the army

60 Being a soldier was a good career, if you didn't get killed! Roman soldiers were well paid and cared for. The empire needed troops to defend its land against attack, and soldiers were well trained. Good fighters were promoted and received extra pay. When they retired they were given money or land.

61 Roman troops carried three main weapons. They fought with javelins, swords and daggers. Each man had to buy his own set, and look after them carefully – one day, his life might depend on them.

62 Soldiers needed many skills. On arrival at a new base they set up camps of tents, but soon afterwards built permanent forts defended by strong walls. Each legion contained men with a wide range of skills, such as cooks, builders, doctors, carpenters, blacksmiths and engineers – but they all had to fight!

▶ Soldiers used their shields to make a protective shell called a *testudo*, or 'tortoise'.

◀ Roman soldiers used the *gladius*, a stabbing sword about 80 centimetres long.

◄ The ballista was a weapon that could hurl a heavy javelin accurately over a range of 500 metres.

63 **The army could march up to 30 kilometres in a day.** When they were hurrying to put down a rebellion, or moving from fort to fort, soldiers travelled quickly, on foot. Troops marched along straight, well-made army roads. Each soldier had to carry a heavy pack containing weapons, armour, tools, cooking pots, food and spare clothes.

64 **The army contained citizens and 'helpers'.** Roman citizens joined the regular army. Men who were not citizens could also fight for Rome. They were known as auxiliaries (helpers) and were organized into special units of their own.

◄ Roman cavalry were usually auxiliary troops raised from non-Roman peoples.

65 **Soldiers worshipped their own special god.** At forts and army camps, soldiers built temples where they honoured the god Mithras, who they believed protected them and gave them life after death.

Ruled by Rome

66 More than 50 million people were ruled by Rome. Celts, Germans, Iberians, and many other peoples lived in territories held by Rome's armies. They had their own languages, customs and beliefs. Rome sent governors to force conquered peoples to pay Roman taxes and obey Roman laws.

▼ The Roman city of Londinium (London) was built where a bridge could be built over the wide River Thames.

67 A few conquered kings and queens did not accept Roman rule. In AD 60 Boudicca, queen of the Iceni tribe of eastern England, led a rebellion against the Romans in Britain. Her army marched on London and other cities but was defeated by Roman soldiers.

▼ British warriors led by Queen Boudicca destroyed London and killed everyone they found.

LOOK LIKE A CELTIC WARRIOR!

Roman writers reported how Celtic warriors decorated their faces and bodies with patterns before going into battle. They believed that the paint was magic, and would protect them. The Celts used a deep-blue dye made from a plant called woad. Ask an adult if you have some special face-painting make-up, then try using it to make up some scary war-paint designs of your own.

68

Cleopatra used beauty and charm to stop the Romans invading. Cleopatra was queen of Egypt and she knew that the Egyptian army would not be able to defeat Roman soldiers. Two Roman army generals, Julius Caesar and Mark Antony, fell in love with Cleopatra. She prevented the Romans invading for many years, but Egypt was eventually conquered.

▶ Queen Cleopatra shown wearing the traditional clothing of an Egyptian queen.

▼ This map shows the Roman Empire in brown, and the roads that they built in black.

69

Romans built monuments to celebrate their victories. Trajan, who ruled from AD 98–117, was a Roman soldier who became emperor. After his army conquered Dacia (now Romania) in AD 106, he gave orders for a 30-metre-high stone pillar to be built in the Forum in Rome. The pillar was decorated with carvings of 2500 Roman soldiers winning wars. It still stands today and is known as Trajan's Column.

The farming life

70 **Rome relied on farmers.** Most Romans lived in the countryside and worked on farms. Farmers produced food for city-dwellers. Food was grown on big estates by teams of slaves, and on small peasant farms where single families worked together.

71 **Farm produce was imported from all over the empire.** Wool and honey came from Britain, wine from Greece, and 400,000 tonnes of wheat were shipped across the Mediterranean Sea from Egypt every year. It was ground into flour, which was used to make bread, the Romans' basic food.

▼ A relief showing a merchant taking delivery of large pottery amphorae (tall jugs or jars) filled with oil or wine.

▲ Slaves work the land on a large Roman estate.

72 **Roman grapes grew on trees.** Vines (climbing plants that produce grapes) were planted among fruit trees in orchards. The trees provided support for the vine stems, and welcome shade to stop the grapes getting scorched by the sun. Grapes were one of the most important crops on Roman farms. The ripe fruits were picked and dried to become raisins, or pulped and made into wine.

73

The most valuable fruit was small, hard, green and bitter! Olives could be pickled in salty water to eat with bread and cheese, or crushed to provide oil. The Romans used olive oil as a medicine, for cooking and preserving food, for cleaning and softening the skin, and even for burning in lamps.

74

Farmers didn't have machines to help them. Heavy work was done by animals or humans, and ploughs were pulled by oxen. Crops were harvested by men and women using sickles (curved knives) and loaded onto carts by hand. Donkeys turned mill wheels to crush olives, grind grain, and to raise drinking water from wells.

KEY

1. Beehives for honey
2. Treading grapes for wine
3. Owner of the farm
4. Vineyard and orchard
5. Threshing wheat
6. Sheep kept in fields
7. Pressing olives
8. Farmworkers harvesting grain
9. Vegetable patch

▶ This mosaic shows dates being harvested.

TRUE OR FALSE?

1. The Romans imported wool and honey from Britain.

2. A raisin is a dried olive.

3. The Romans used olive oil as a medicine.

Answers:
1. True 2. False 3. True

37

Work like a slave

75 In Rome not all people were equal. How you were treated in society depended on your class. Free-born people (citizens) had rights that were guaranteed by law – for example, to travel or find work. Citizens could vote in elections, and receive free food handouts. Slaves had very few rights. They belonged to their owners just like dogs or horses.

76 Slaves were purchased from slave-traders or born to slave parents. People could also be condemned to slavery as a punishment for a serious crime, or if they were captured in a war.

▼ Slaves were bought and sold at slave-markets. They were paraded before the citizens to be chosen or rejected. The slaves could not leave, or choose what work to do. They could be cruelly punished, neglected or given away.

◀ Slaves at work in a Roman mosaic from about the year AD 500. They were expected to wear simple tunics.

77 Slaves were trained to do all sorts of tasks. They did everything their owners demanded, from looking after children to hard labour on farms. Many slaves were trusted by their owners, who valued their skills. A few slaves became respected chefs or doctors.

78 Sometimes slaves were set free by their owners. Freedom could be a reward for loyalty or long service. Some sick or dying slave-owners gave orders that their slaves should be freed. They did not want their slaves to pass to a new owner who might treat them badly.

79 Some slaves did very well after they were freed. Former slaves used the skills they had learned to set up businesses of their own. Many were successful, and a few became very rich.

Roman know-how

80 The Romans pioneered new building materials and designs. They discovered concrete, which was much cheaper and easier to use than stone. They baked clay at high temperatures to make long-lasting bricks. They used arches to create tall, strong walls and doorways. They designed massive domes for buildings that were too big to be roofed with wooden beams.

81 Aqueducts brought 750 million litres of fresh water to the city of Rome every day. This water was carried by pipes to public fountains and rich people's homes.

▼ The Romans were amazing builders and architects. Their roads and many of their buildings have lasted more than 2000 years.

I DON'T BELIEVE IT!

Our word 'plumber' comes from *plumbum*, the Latin word for the lead used by Romans to make water pipes. The same word is also used for a 'plumb-line', still in use today.

◀ Romans used valves to pump water uphill. Water would then come out of fountains.

84 Even the best doctors often failed to cure their patients. But Roman doctors were skilled at sewing up cuts and joining broken bones. They also used herbs for medicines and painkillers.

Spatula
Used to mix medicines

82 No one improved on the Roman's water supplies until the 1800s! They invented pumps with valves to pump water uphill. This went into high tanks above fountains. Gravity pulled the water out of the fountain's spout.

Forceps
Used to extract small items from wounds

Spoon
Used to give medicines to patients

Hook
Used to probe wounds

83 Despite their advanced technology, Romans believed that illness was caused by witchcraft. To find a cure, they made a special visit to a temple, to ask the gods with healing powers to make them better.

▶ Roman surgeons carried a standard kit of equipment that could be used to treat patients and deal with different types of injuries.

Prayers and sacrifices

▼ The marriage of Jupiter and Juno, watched by Roma the patron goddess of the city of Rome.

Juno
Queen of the gods and patron of marriage

Jupiter
King of the gods and god of the sky

Minerva
Goddess of the arts and of wisdom, daughter of Jupiter

Neptune
God of rivers, the sea and earthquakes, brother of Jupiter

Mars
God of warfare and peace treaties, ancestor of the Roman people

Venus
Represented love and beauty, like the Greek goddess Aphrodite

Apollo
Greek god of arts, light and prophecy, worshipped in Rome from 430 BC

Diana
Goddess of hunting, the moon and childbirth, daughter of Jupiter

Vulcan
God of fire and blacksmiths, husband of Venus, son of Jupiter

Vesta
Goddess of home and family, her temple had an eternal flame

Mercury
God of business, money and travel, messenger of the gods

Ceres
Goddess of grain crops and farmers, sister of Jupiter

85 **The Romans had many gods.** There were gods of the city, the country, and of the underworld, and some were worshipped by people of certain professions. The Romans even adopted gods from other countries that were part of the empire. Ideas and gods from Greece had a very big impact.

86 **The emperor was also chief priest.** As part of his duties he said prayers and offered sacrifices to the gods who protected Rome. His title was *pontifex maximus* (chief bridge-builder) because people believed he acted as a bridge between the gods and ordinary people.

87 **Families made offerings to the gods every day.** They left food, wine and incense in front of a shrine in their house. A shrine is like a mini temple. It contained statues of ancient gods called the *lares* and *penates*. The *lares* were ancestor spirits who looked after living family members. The *penates* guarded the family's food.

I DON'T BELIEVE IT!

After an animal had been sacrificed to the gods, a priest, called a *haruspex*, examined its liver. If it was diseased, bad luck was on the way!

▲ A Roman pours a libation (small offering) to the gods, onto the ground at a temple.

88 **Romans were superstitious.** They decorated their homes with magic symbols, and children were made to wear good-luck charms. They thought they could foretell the future by observing animals – bees were a sign of riches but a hooting owl foretold danger.

89 **Some of the first Christians lived in Rome.** For years Christianity was banned in Rome, so Christians met secretly in catacombs (underground passages). They also used the catacombs as burial places. The persecution of Christians ended after 313, and in 380 Christianity became the official state religion of Rome.

On the move

90 Rome was at the hub of a network of roads that stretched for more than 85,000 kilometres. It had been built to link outlying parts of the empire to the capital, so that Roman armies or government officials could travel quickly. To make travel as quick as possible, roads were built in straight lines, taking the shortest route.

▲ A street in Pompeii. The stepping stones were provided so people could cross without treading in horse droppings and rubbish.

91 Rome's first main road was built in 312 BC. Its name was the Via Appia (*via* is the Latin word for 'road'). It ran from Rome to the port of Brundisium on the south-east coast of Italy. Many travellers from Greece arrived there, and the new road made their journey to Rome quicker and easier.

92 Some Roman roads have survived for over 2000 years. Each road was made of layers of earth and stones on top of a firm, flat foundation. It was surfaced with stone slabs or gravel. The centre had a camber (curved surface), so that rainwater drained away into ditches on either side.

▶ Trained men worked out the route, and slaves did the heavy labour. Army roads were built by soldiers.

Route accurately marked out

Solid foundations

Drainage ditch

Large surface slabs

93 Engineers used special tools to help them make accurate surveys. They made careful plans and took measurements before starting any building project, such as a new road or city walls.

▼ These engineers are using a *groma* to measure straight lines on a road.

94 Poor people walked everywhere. They couldn't afford to hire a horse or donkey, or a carriage pulled by oxen. With luck they could hitch a lift in a farm wagon – but it wouldn't be a comfortable ride!

I DON'T BELIEVE IT!
The Romans often consulted a fortune-teller or a priest before even setting out on a long journey.

95 Town streets were crowded and dirty. Rich people travelled in curtained beds called litters, carried by slaves. Stepping stones allowed ordinary people to avoid the mud and rubbish underfoot.

96 Heavy loads often travelled by water. There were no lorries in Roman times. Ships, powered by sails and by slaves rowing, carried people and cargo over water. But water-transport was slow, and could be dangerous. Roman ships were often attacked by pirates, and shipwrecks were common.

◄ A Roman war galley. The ram at the bow could be used to sink enemy ships, or the soldiers might fight their way on board enemy ships.

Uncovering the past

97 **Lots of evidence survives to tell us about Roman times.** Archaeologists have discovered the remains of many Roman buildings, from palaces and aqueducts, to temples, hospitals and homes. They have also found works of art, coins, jewellery, pottery, glass, and many tools and objects used in daily life.

98 **The oceans contain secrets from the past.** Marine archaeology is the hunt for amazing relics under the sea. Many Roman shipwrecks have been discovered in the Mediterranean Sea, including a wine carrier with 6000 amphorae off the coast near Marseilles in France.

▼ Archaeologists find a Roman pot in the bed of the Ljubljanica River in Slovenia. Underwater techniques are relatively new and have allowed archaeologists to make dramatic discoveries.

▼ A mosaic preserved at Herculaneum shows Roman gods.

QUIZ

1. What does the name Marcus mean?
2. Which of these things would not be discovered by an archaeologist studying ancient Rome: glass, telephone, coin?
3. What is marine archaeology?

Answers:
1. God of War 2. A telephone
3. The study of relics underwater

▼ Roman coins have survived in large numbers allowing us to study emperors and gods.

99 Until the 20th century, grand, important buildings were often planned and decorated in Roman style. Architects believed that Roman designs inspired respect, so many cities have churches, museums, art galleries, colleges and even banks that look like Roman temples or Roman villas.

100 Roman names are still quite common. In some parts of the world, children are given Roman names or names based on Latin words. These include Amanda (Loveable), Diana (Moon Goddess), Patricia (Noble), Laura (Laurel-tree), Marcus (God of War), Victor (Winner), and Vincent (Conqueror).

▲ Casts of bodies found in Pompeii. The casts are made by pouring plaster into hollow spaces left in the volcanic ash where bodies have rotted away.

Index

Page numbers in **bold** refer to main entries, those in *italics* refer to illustrations

A

amphitheatre 7, 29
Anthony, Mark 35
apartments 11, *11*
aqueducts 7, 9, *9*, 40, 46
archaeology **46**, *46*
army 31, **32–33**, 44
Augustus 31
Aurelian Wall 7, *9*

B

ballista *32–33*
baths 7, **24–25**, *24, 25*
boots 21
Boudicca 34, *34*
boys 16, *16*, 19, 23
building technology 40–41, 45

C

Caesar, Julius 8, 30, *30*, 31, 35
Caligula 31
Capitoline Hill 8
cavalry *33*
central heating 11, *11*
chariot racing 29, *29*
Christianity 43
Circus Maximus *6*, 29
citizens 8, 20, 33, 38
Cleopatra 35, *35*
clothes **20–21**, *20, 21*
coins *31*, 46, *47*
Colosseum 7, 29, *29*
combs 23, *23*
Curia Julia *8*

D

dancing 27
doctors **41**
drains 9
drink 14

E

eating 15, *15*
education 16–17
elections 30, 38
emperors 30, 31, *31*, 42, 47

F

families **18–19**, 43
farming **36–37**
fashion 20–21, 22

F

fire brigade 11
fish *15*
food 13, **14–15**, 36
Forum 7, 8
fruit 14, *14*, 37
funerals 19

G

games 27, *27*
girls 16, 19
gladiators 7, **28**, *28*, 29
gladius *32*
glass *14*
gods 33, 41, **42–43**, *42*, 47
government 7, 8, 30 31
grapes *14*, 36

H

hairstyles 22, *22*, 23
herbs *15*
homes **10–11**, *10, 11*, 18, 46

I J

Imperial Palace *6*
imports 36
ink 17
Italy *6*
jewellery *13*, *23*, 46

L

lavatories 9
law courts 8
laws 31
Londinium (London) 34, *34*

M

make-up 22
markets 7, 13, *13*
masks 27, *27*
meals 14
meat 15
merchants 12, *36*
mosaics 11, *39*
music 27

N O

names 47
Nero 30, 31
nobles 8
Octavian 31, *31*
olives *15*, 37

P

palaces 46
perfumes 23, 24

P

pets 19
plays 26
plebians 8
plumbing 41
Pompeii 10, *44*, 47
Pont Du Gard *9*

R

reading 16, 17
religion 7, 26, 42–43
republic 30
River Tiber 6, *6*
roads 44–45
Roman Empire 6, 12, 32, **34–35**, *35*, 44
Rome **6–7**, *6–7*, **8–9**, *8–9*
Romulus and Remus 30, *30*
rulers **30–31**

S

sandals 21, *21*
school **16–17**
Senate 8
senators 20
Servian Wall 7, *9*
sewers 9
ships 12, *12*, 45, *45*, 46
shops 11, **13**, *13*, 25
slaves 8, 11, 14, *15*, 16, 22, 36, *36*, **38–39**, *38, 39*, 44, 45
soldiers **32–33**, *32–33*, *44*
spices *15*
sports 7, 24
superstitions 43
surgical equipment *41*

T

temples *6*, 7, 8, 33, 41, 43, 46, 47
testudo 32–33
theatre **26–27**, *26–27*
toga 20, *20*, 21
trade 11, **12–13**, 17
Trajan *31*, 35
travel **44–45**

V W

vegetables *15*
villas 10, 47
walls *8–9*, **9**
water supplies 41, *41*
weapons **32**, *32–33*, 33, *33*
wedding *18*
wine 14, 36, 46
writing 16–17, *16*